THE LITTLE

GREEN BOOK

THE LITTLE GREEN BOOK

Cherry Denman

EBURY PRESS LONDON

First published in Great Britain in 1990
by Ebury Press Limited
an imprint of the Random Century Group
20 Vauxhall Bridge Road
London SW1V 2SA

~ Printed and bound in Italy ~

ISBN O 85223 897 5

~ WITH THANKS TO ~
Mark and Mindy Lucas
for saying it was a good idea ~
Alexandra Denman, Kate Westgarth & Chris Thomson
for saying they could help ~
Gail Rebuck
for saying yes ~
Joanna Roughton
for saying everything was fine
and
Charlie and Freddie
for saying nothing at all.

THIS BOOK IS
DEDICATED
TO
THE
ASH
HAZEL
POPLAR
MULBERRY

THE CONTENTS

THE SEEDLING

THE SAPLING

THE TREE

THE FRUITING

THE FALLING OF LEAVES

THE
SEEDLING

THERE'S MUSIC IN THE
WAKING WOODS
THERE'S GLORY IN THE AIR~

John Clare
Impulses of Spring.

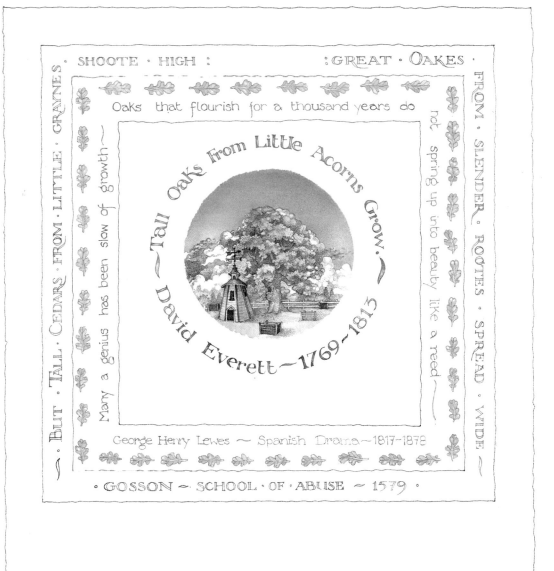

SHOOTE · HIGH :   : GREAT · OAKES

LITTLE · GRAYNES ~

FROM · LITTLE ·

BUT · TALL · CEDARS · FROM · LITTLE · GRAYNES

Oaks that flourish for a thousand years do

Many a genius has been slow of growth ~

~ Tall Oaks From Little Acorns Grow ·

· David Everett — 1769~1813

not spring up into beauty like a reed ~

FROM · SLENDER · ROOTES · SPREAD · WIDE ~

George Henry Lewes ~ Spanish Drama ~ 1817-1878

· GOSSON ~ SCHOOL · OF · ABUSE ~ 1579 ·

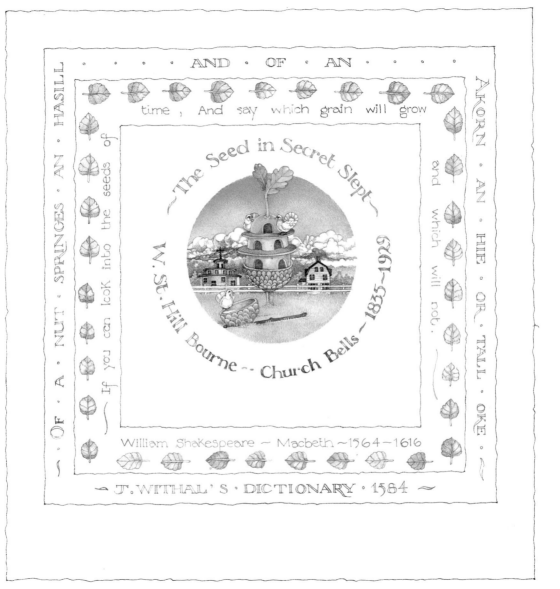

AND · OF · AN

time , And say which grain will grow

HASILL · AN · SPRINGES · A · NUT · OF · A

AKORN · AN · HIE · OR · TALL · OKE

If you can look into the seeds of

and which will not .

~ The Seed in Secret Slept ~

W · St · Hill Bourne -- Church Bells - 1835-1929

William Shakespeare ~ Macbeth ~1564-1616

~ J · WITHAL'S · DICTIONARY · 1584 ~

JOB·12·8

SPEAK TO THE EARTH, AND IT SHALL TEACH THEE·

THE TREE OF MAN WAS NEVER QUIET

A. E. HOUSMAN
A shropshire lad
XXXI

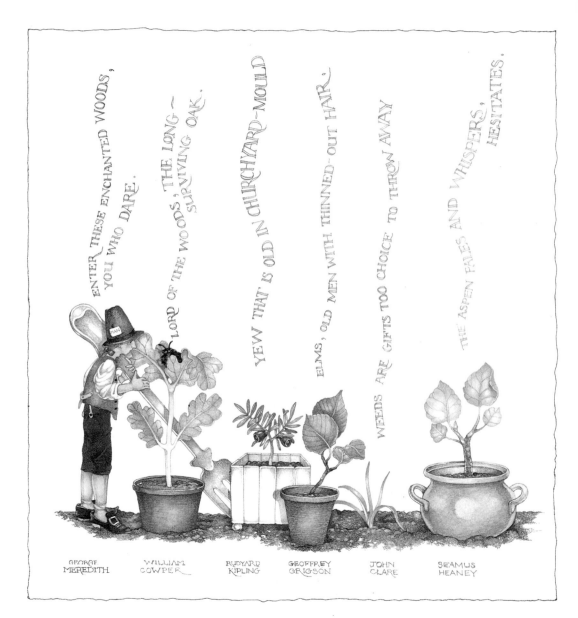

ENTER THESE ENCHANTED WOODS, YOU WHO DARE.

LORD OF THE WOODS, THE LONG-SURVIVING OAK.

YEW THAT IS OLD IN CHURCHYARD-MOULD

ELMS, OLD MEN WITH THINNED-OUT HAIR,

WEEDS ARE GIFTS TOO CHOICE TO THROW AWAY

THE ASPEN PALES AND WHISPERS, HESITATES.

GEORGE
MEREDITH

WILLIAM
COWPER

RUDYARD
KIPLING

GEOFFREY
GRIGSON

JOHN
CLARE

SEAMUS
HEANEY

THE HOLLY BEARS A PRICKLE, AS SHARP AS ANY THORN,

WHAT IS A WEED? A PLANT WHOSE VIRTUES HAVE NOT BEEN DISCOVERED.

THE SHARP, DARK EXCLAMATION MARK OF A CYPRESS.

THE SYCAMORE, CAPRICIOUS IN ATTIRE,

LET THEM CONSUME AWAY LIKE A SNAIL

ANON

RALPH WALDO EMERSON

LETTICE COOPER

WILLIAM COWPER

THE BOOK OF COMMON PRAYER

L'EMBARRAS DES RICHESSES.
THE MORE ALTERNATIVES,
THE MORE DIFFICULT THE CHOICE.

Abbé D'Allainval
Title of Comedy

IS THERE IN THE WORLD
A CLIMATE MORE UNCERTAIN
THAN OUR OWN?

William Congreve
Amendments of Mr. Collier's False and Imperfect
Citations.

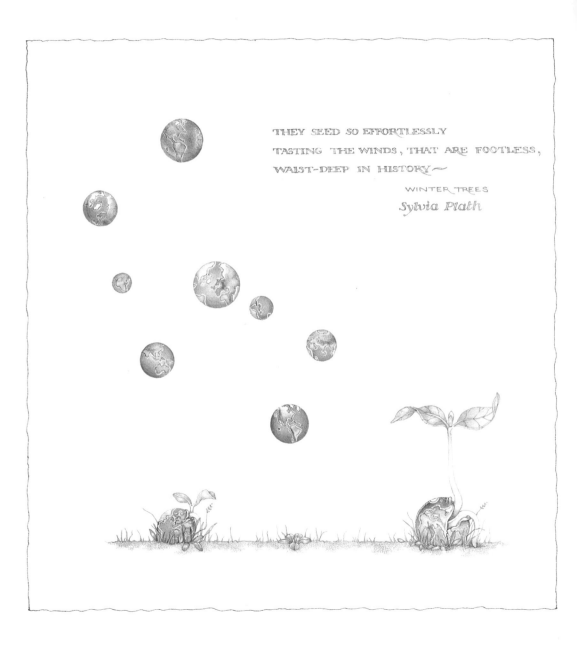

THEY SEED SO EFFORTLESSLY
TASTING THE WINDS, THAT ARE FOOTLESS,
WAIST-DEEP IN HISTORY ~

WINTER TREES
Sylvia Plath

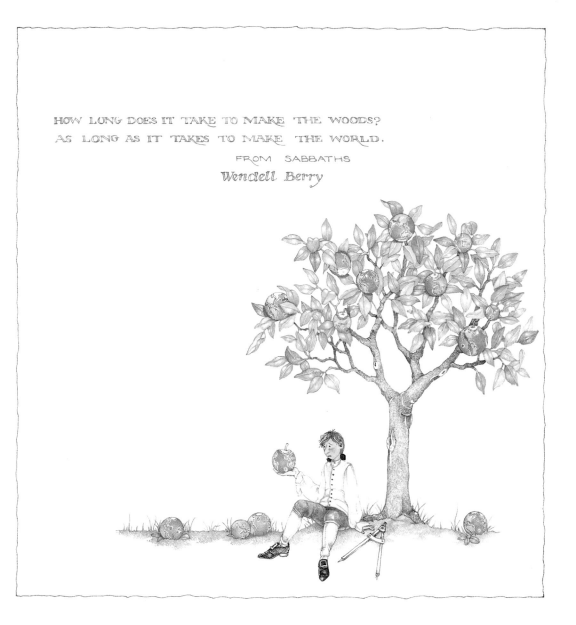

HOW LONG DOES IT TAKE TO MAKE THE WOODS?
AS LONG AS IT TAKES TO MAKE THE WORLD.
FROM SABBATHS
Wendell Berry

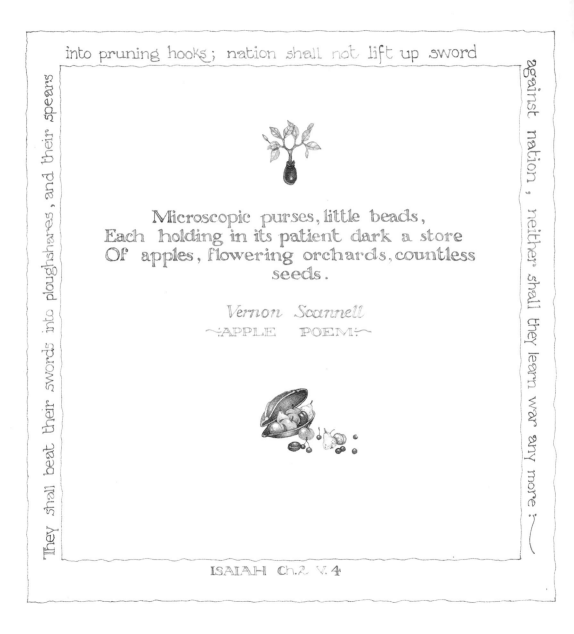

into pruning hooks; nation shall not lift up sword

against nation, neither shall they learn war any more:—

They shall beat their swords into ploughshares, and their spears

Microscopic purses, little beads,
Each holding in its patient dark a store
Of apples, flowering orchards, countless
seeds.

Vernon Scannell
APPLE POEM

ISAIAH Ch.2 V.4

two blades of grass to grow upon a spot of ground where only one grew

before, would deserve better of mankind, and do more essential service to

his country than the whole race of politicians put together:~

And he gave it for his opinion, that whoever could make two ears of corn or

GULLIVER'S TRAVELS   JONATHAN SWIFT

VOYAGE TO BROBDINGNAG

THE
SAPLING

AS THE SAP RISES IN THE TREES
AS THE SAP PAINTS THE TREES A
VIOLENT GREEN
SO RISES THE WRATH OF NATURE'S
CREATURES
AT MAN

—ALONE IN THE WOODS—
Stevie Smith

WHAT IS ALL THIS JUICE AND ALL THIS JOY?
A STRAIN OF THE EARTH'S SWEET BEING
IN THE BEGINNING
IN EDEN GARDEN ~ HAVE, GET, BEFORE
IT CLOY.

~Spring~
Gerard Manley Hopkins

EVERY GREEN WAS YOUNG, EVERY PORE
WAS OPEN, AND EVERY STALK WAS
SWOLLEN WITH RACING CURRENTS OF
JUICE.

~ Far From The Madding Crowd ~
Thomas Hardy

AND·FIRE·GREEN·AS·GRASS
DYLAN·THOMAS·
SHADE
THOUGHT·IN·A·GREEN·
·TO·A·GREEN·
ANDREW·MARVELL
·THE·GARDEN·
·MADE·
·AND·DYING·
·TIME·HELD·ME·GREEN·
ANNIHILATING·ALL·THAT'S

A · PERFECT · FIRE · OF · GREEN ·
R · L · STEVENSON ·

· AND · THIS · TREE · IS · GREEN · FIRE · IN · A · WORLD · OF · TREES ·
ALMOST · SUMMER · IN · THE · HEART · OF · THE · WOODS ·

· PETER · LEVI ·

· COLLECTED POEMS ·

GHOSTS OF THE WORLD-WOOD : THE TREES ARE FELLED,
STUMPS ; PUNY SAPLINGS WHICH REPLACE THEM
WILL OUTGROW ME AND THEN OUTLIVE ME.

~ THE THICKET ~
MICHAEL VINCE

THE TREES ARE COMING INTO LEAF
LIKE SOMETHING ALMOST BEING SAID;
THE RECENT BUDS RELAX AND SPREAD,
THEIR GREENNESS IS A KIND OF GRIEF.

~ THE TREES ~
PHILIP LARKIN

THEN·NATURE·APPROACHED·ME, CALLING·ME·BY·MY· NAME; AND·HE·BADE·ME·TAKE·HEED, AND·GATHER· WISDOM·FROM·ALL·THE·WONDERS·OF·THE·WORLD.'

Piers the Ploughman · William Langland

AND·FLOWERING·SHEAF, AND · I · WILL· HOLD

YOU, ROOT ·AND · FRUIT·AND·FALLEN · LEAF.

AND·FLOWERING·SHEAF, AND · I · WILL· HOLD

I · WILL · UPHOLD · YOU, TRUNK·AND·SHOOT,

E. J. Scovell.

I read, and sigh, and wish I were a tree—
For sure then I should grow
To fruit or shade; at least some bird
would trust
Her household to me, and I should be
just.

~THE TEMPLE. AFFLICTION.~
GEORGE HERBERT

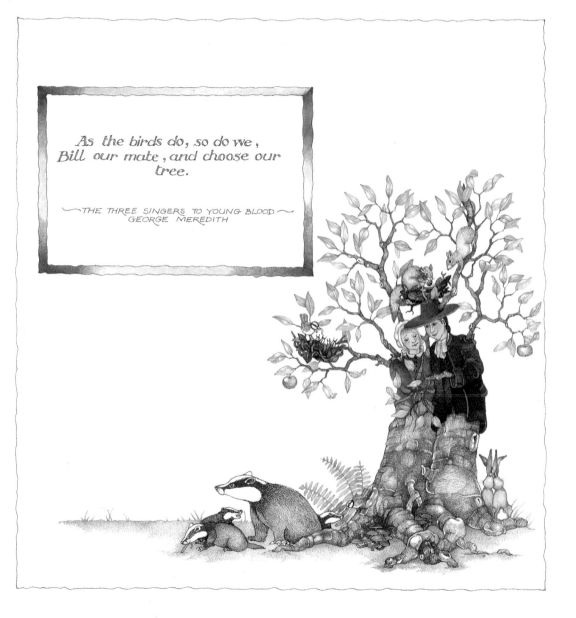

As the birds do, so do we,
Bill our mate, and choose our
tree.

~ THE THREE SINGERS TO YOUNG BLOOD ~
GEORGE MEREDITH

ROBERT HERRICK

NEW THINGS SUCCEED, AS FORMER
THINGS GROW OLD.

Ceremonies for Candlemasse Eve

THE TREE.

AND · THE · LEAVES · OF · THE · TREE
WERE · FOR · THE · HEALING · OF ·
· THE · NATIONS ·

The Revelation of
St. John the Divine

xxii. 2

I SEE MEN AS TREES,
WALKING.

St. Mark
VIII 24

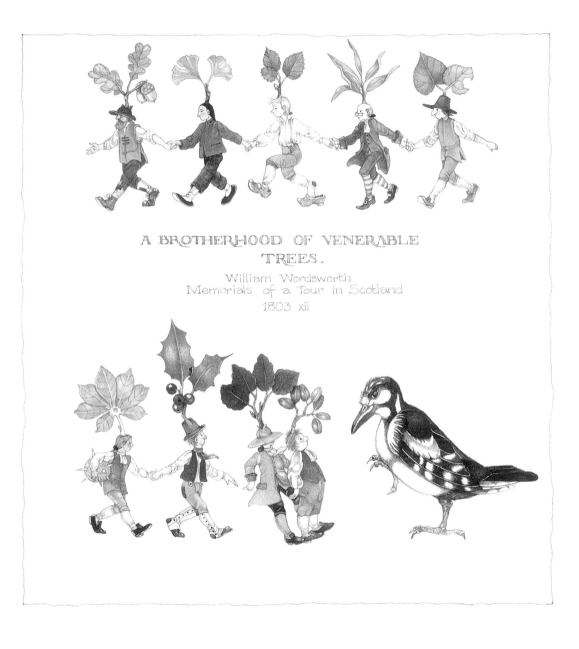

A BROTHERHOOD OF VENERABLE
TREES.

William Wordsworth
Memorials of a Tour in Scotland
1803 xii

OUR MEDDLING INTELLECT

MISSHAPES THE BEAUTEOUS FORMS

LORE WHICH NATURE BRINGS;

OF THINGS. SWEET IS THE

One impulse from a vernal wood
May teach you more of man,
Of moral evil and of good,
Than all the sages can.

The Tables Turned.
William Wordsworth.

OF THINGS, LET

COME FORTH INTO THE LIGHT

NATURE BE YOUR TEACHER.

TRA LA

Trees that for twenty thousand
years
Your vows have kept,
You have suddenly healed the pain
of a traveller's heart,
And moved his brush to write a
new song
Chang Fang-Sheng 4th Century

WORDSWORTH

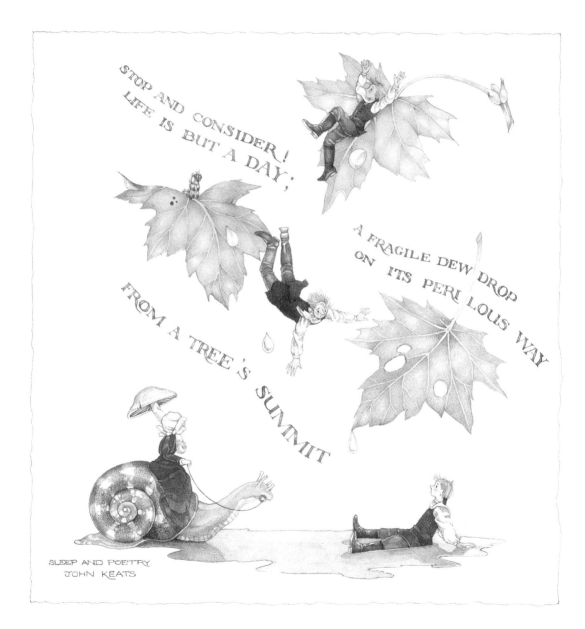

STOP AND CONSIDER!
LIFE IS BUT A DAY;

A FRAGILE DEW DROP
ON ITS PERILOUS WAY

FROM A TREE'S SUMMIT

SLEEP AND POETRY
JOHN KEATS

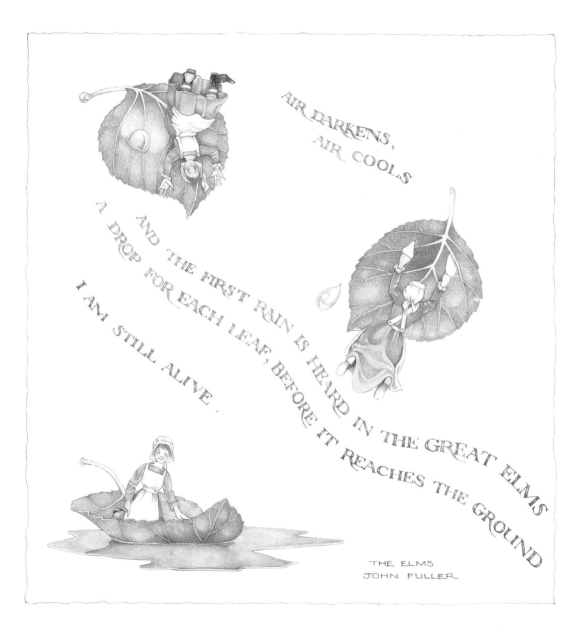

AIR DARKENS,
AIR COOLS

AND THE FIRST RAIN IS HEARD IN THE GREAT ELMS

A DROP FOR EACH LEAF, BEFORE IT REACHES THE GROUND

I AM STILL ALIVE.

THE ELMS
JOHN FULLER

A FOOL SEES NOT THE SAME TREE THAT A WISE
MAN SEES.

WILLIAM BLAKE
PROVERBS OF HELL

THE TREE WHICH MOVES SOME TO TEARS OF
JOY IS IN THE EYES OF OTHERS ONLY A GREEN
THING WHICH STANDS IN THE WAY...

WILLIAM BLAKE
IN A LETTER TO THE REV. DR.
TRUSLER

I THINK THAT I SHALL NEVER SEE
A BILLBOARD LOVELY AS A TREE.
INDEED, UNLESS THE BILLBOARDS FALL
I'LL NEVER SEE A TREE AT ALL.

Song of the Open Road
OGDEN NASH

POEMS ARE MADE BY FOOLS LIKE ME,
BUT ONLY GOD CAN MAKE A TREE.

Trees
Poems, Essays & Letters
Joyce Kilmer

So
Architects do square
and hew,
Green trees that in
the forest grew.

A Dialogue between
the Soul and Body

ANDREW MARVELL

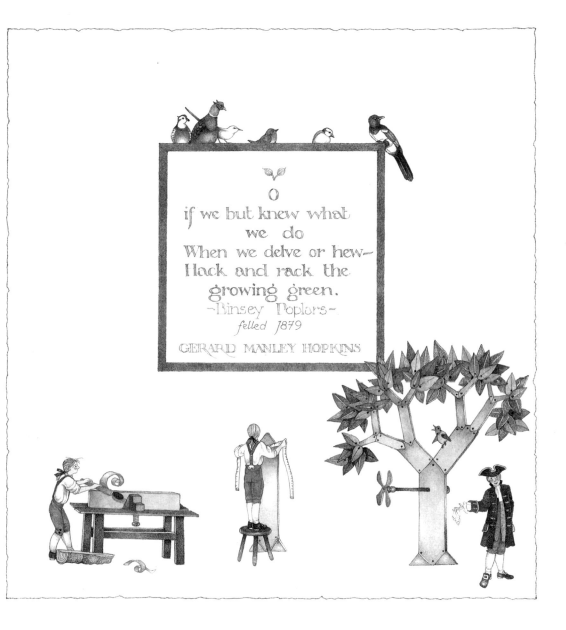

O
if we but knew what
we do
When we delve or hew—
Hack and rack the
growing green.
~Binsey Poplars~
felled 1879

GERARD MANLEY HOPKINS

ASH AND OAK, CHESTNUT
AND YEW;
WITNESSES, HUGE, MILD
BEINGS WHO SUFFER THE
CONSEQUENCE
OF SHARING OUR PLANET
AND CANNOT MOVE
AWAY FROM ANY EVIL
WE
SUBJECT THEM TO,

Trees
Ruth Fainlight

THE

FRUITING

WHAT WONDROUS LIFE IS THIS I LEAD!
RIPE APPLES DROP ABOUT MY HEAD;
THE LUSCIOUS CLUSTERS OF THE VINE
UPON MY MOUTH DO CRUSH THEIR WINE;
THE NECTARINE, AND CURIOUS PEACH
INTO MY HANDS THEMSELVES DO REACH;
STUMBLING ON MELONS, AS I PASS
ENSNARED WITH FLOWERS, I FALL ON
GRASS.

Andrew Marvell
THE GARDEN

I HAD A LITTLE NUT TREE,
NOTHING WOULD IT BEAR
BUT A SILVER NUTMEG
AND A GOLDEN PEAR.

NURSERY RHYME

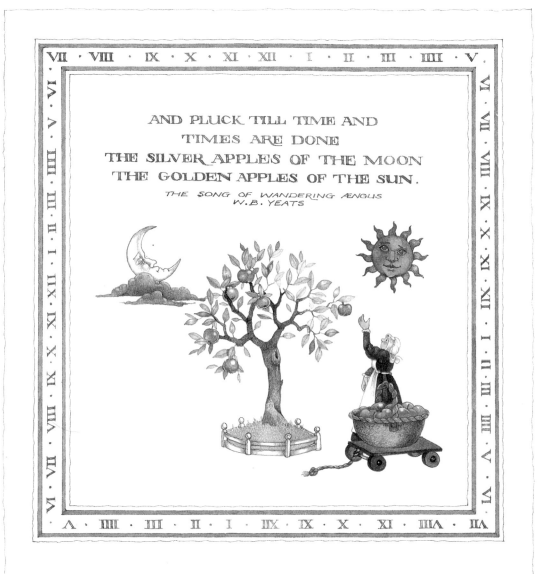

AND PLUCK TILL TIME AND
TIMES ARE DONE
THE SILVER APPLES OF THE MOON
THE GOLDEN APPLES OF THE SUN.

THE SONG OF WANDERING ÆNGUS
W.B. YEATS

BUT APPLES PLANTS OF SUCH A PRICE,
NO TREE COULD EVER BEAR THEM TWICE.

Bermudas
Andrew Marvell

...BESPANGLED AND GORGEOUSLY APPARELLED
WITH GREEN LEAVES, BLOOMS AND GOODLY
FRUITS AS WITH A RICH ROBE OF
EMBROIDERED WORK...

A Treatise of Fruit Trees
Ralph Austen

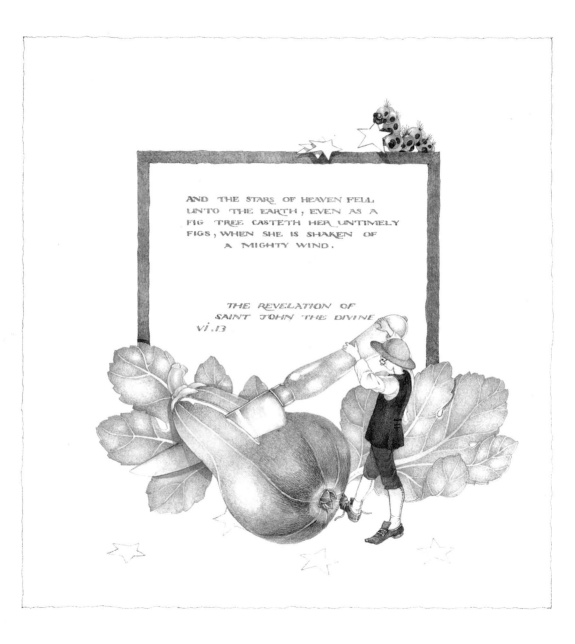

AND THE STARS OF HEAVEN FELL
UNTO THE EARTH, EVEN AS A
FIG TREE CASTETH HER UNTIMELY
FIGS, WHEN SHE IS SHAKEN OF
A MIGHTY WIND.

THE REVELATION OF
SAINT JOHN THE DIVINE
VI. 13

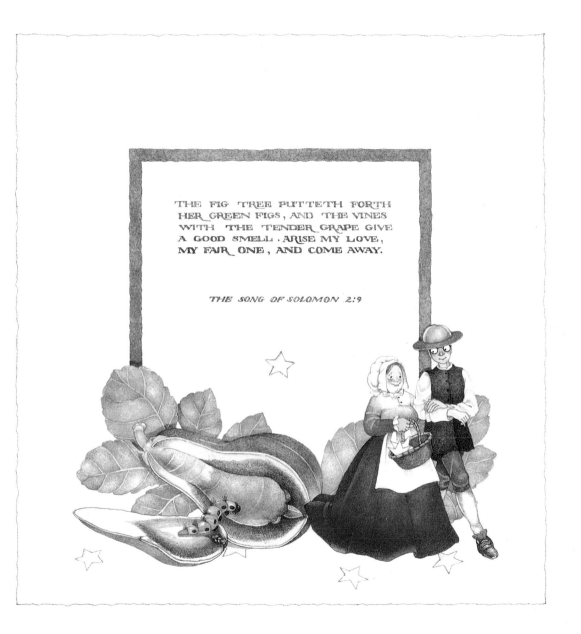

THE FIG TREE PUTTETH FORTH
HER GREEN FIGS, AND THE VINES
WITH THE TENDER GRAPE GIVE
A GOOD SMELL . ARISE MY LOVE,
MY FAIR ONE, AND COME AWAY.

THE SONG OF SOLOMON 2:9

FROM THE GREENGROCER TREE
YOU GET GRAPES AND GREEN PEA,
CAULIFLOWER, PINEAPPLE, AND
CRANBERRIES

Sir William Schwenk Gilbert

IOLANTHE

ALL HEDGEROWS SHOULD BE PLANTED
WITH FRUIT TREES AND THOSE THAT
PICKED IT TO SATISFY THEIR OWN
HUNGER SHOULD GO UNPUNISHED.

John Tavener

AN APPLE A DAY
KEEPS THE
DOCTOR AWAY.

Go, bind thou up yon dangling apricocks,
Which, like unruly children, make their sire
Stoop with oppression of their prodigal
weight.

WILLIAM SHAKESPEARE ~ KING RICHARD II

CHERRIES KISSING AS THEY GROW,
AND INVITING MEN TO TASTE,

JOHN FLETCHER
LOVE'S EMBLEMS

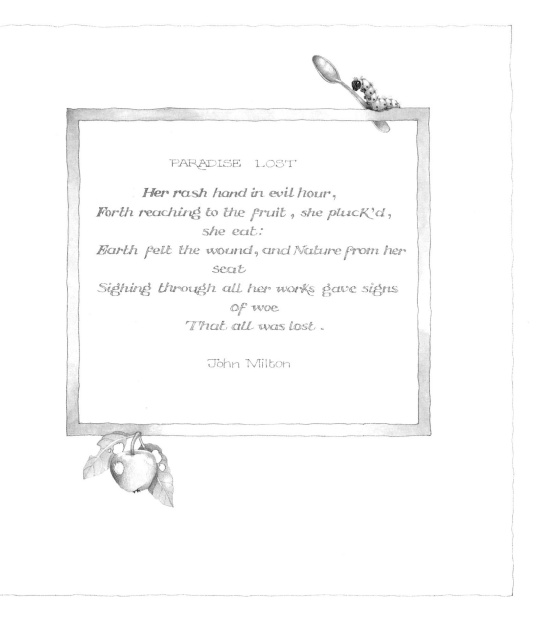

PARADISE LOST

Her rash hand in evil hour,
Forth reaching to the fruit, she pluck'd,
she eat:
Earth felt the wound, and Nature from her
seat
Sighing through all her works gave signs
of woe
That all was lost.

John Milton

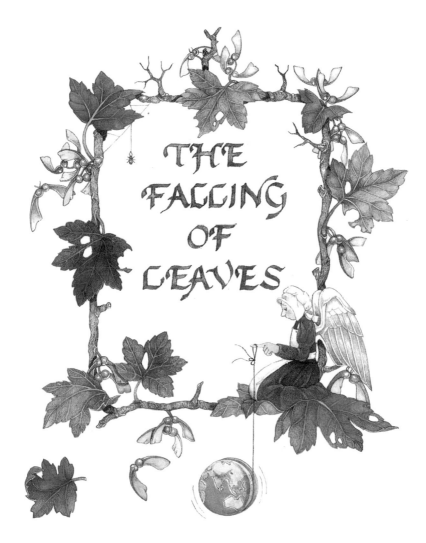

THE
FALLING
OF
LEAVES

THE LEAVES OF LIFE
KEEP FALLING
ONE
BY
ONE.

Omar Khayyám
Edward Fitzgerald

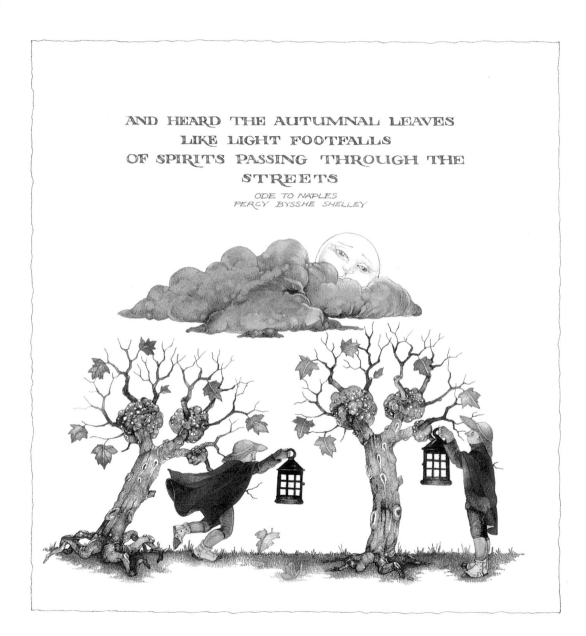

AND HEARD THE AUTUMNAL LEAVES
LIKE LIGHT FOOTFALLS
OF SPIRITS PASSING THROUGH THE
STREETS

ODE TO NAPLES
PERCY BYSSHE SHELLEY

THE SPIRIT OF THE PLACE SEEMED
TO BE ALL ATTENTION; THE WOOD
LISTENED AS I WENT AND HELD ITS
BREATH TO NUMBER MY FOOTFALLS.

*AN AUTUMN EFFECT
ROBERT LOUIS STEVENSON*

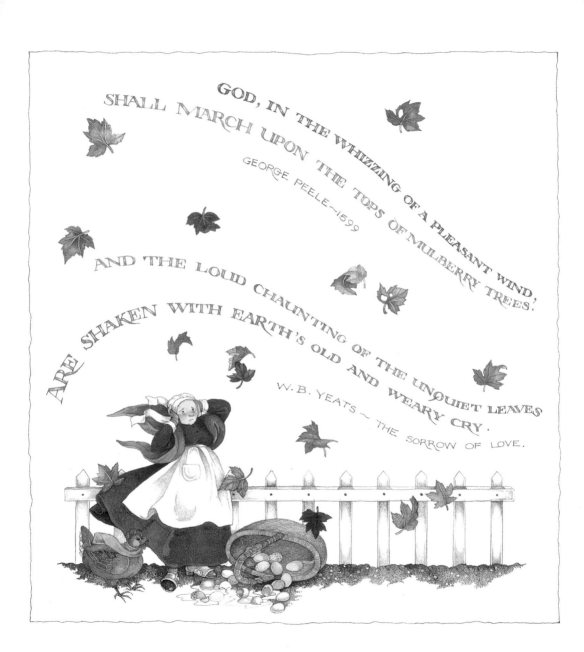

GOD, IN THE WHIZZING OF A PLEASANT WIND,
SHALL MARCH UPON THE TOPS OF MULBERRY TREES.'

GEORGE PEELE ~ 1599

AND THE LOUD CHAUNTING OF THE UNQUIET LEAVES
ARE SHAKEN WITH EARTH'S OLD AND WEARY CRY.

W. B. YEATS ~ THE SORROW OF LOVE.

VAGUE RUMOURS THAT WENT AMONG THE TREETOPS

ROBERT LOUIS STEVENSON ~ AN AUTUMN EFFECT

WHISPERING WINDS THE POPLARS COURTING.

THOMAS BROWN

LEAVES FROM ETERNITY ARE SIMPLE THINGS.
JOHN CLARE

WITHOUT THE COMPANY OF LEAVES...
GILLIAN CLARKE

YOU LEAVES DRENCHED WITH THE LIFEBLOOD
OF THE YEAR ~
C. DAY LEWIS

TREES SCREAM AND DROP THEIR BRIGHT LEAVES.

ALLEN GINSBERG

THE PERISHED LEAVES OF HOPE,

DANTE GABRIEL ROSSETTI

AND WE ALL DO FADE AS A LEAF.

THE BIBLE

ILL FARES THE LAND, TO HAST'NING ILLS
A PREY,
WHERE WEALTH ACCUMULATES, AND MEN
DECAY

OLIVER GOLDSMITH
THE DESERTED VILLAGE

GIVE ME A LAND OF BOUGHS IN LEAF,
A LAND OF TREES THAT STAND;
WHERE TREES ARE FALLEN, THERE IS GRIEF;
I LOVE NO LEAFLESS LAND...

A.E.HOUSMAN

SENSING US, THE TREES TREMBLE IN
THEIR SLEEP,
THE LIVING LEAVES RECOIL BEFORE OUR
FIRES.

KATHLEEN RAINE
LONDON TREES

THE FOREST TURNED
FROM WOOD
TO STONE
TO DUST.

ANTHONY THWAITE
DEAD WOOD

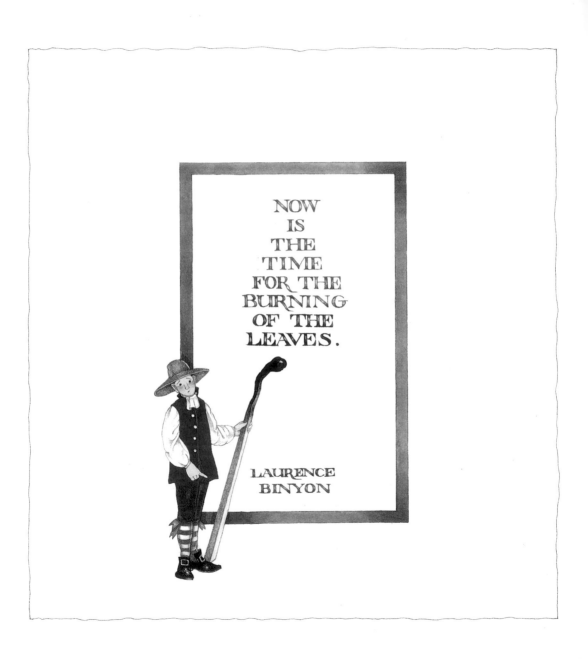

NOW
IS
THE
TIME
FOR THE
BURNING
OF THE
LEAVES.

LAURENCE
BINYON

ACKNOWLEDGEMENTS

Every endeavour has been made to find copyright holders of quotations. Any infringement of copyright is inadvertent, and the publishers should be notified. Acknowledgement is made to the following for quotations used in this book.

'Alone in the Woods' from The Collected Poems of Stevie Smith, Stevie Smith Copyright 1972 Stevie Smith. Reprinted by permission of New Directions Publishing Corporation.

'Apple Poem' from Funeral Games, Vernon Scannell (Robson Books).

'Autumn Gold: New England Fall' from Collected Poems 1947-80, Allen Ginsberg (Penguin Books Ltd).

'The Betrothal' from Collected Poems, E.J. Scovell (Carcanet Press Ltd).

'The Bushy Leaved Oak Tree' from Sweeny Astray - A Version from the Irish, Seamus Heaney (Field Day Publications).

'Cardiff Elms' from Selected Poems, Gillian Clarke (Carcanet Press Ltd).

'Dead Wood' from Poems 1953-83, Anthony Thwaite (Martin Secker & Warburg).

'The Elms' from Cannibals and Missionaries, John Fuller. Reprinted by permission of Martin Secker & Warburg.

'Fenny' Lettice Cooper (Virago Press).

'Fern Hill' from Poems of Dylan Thomas, Dylan Thomas. Copyright 1945 by the Trustees for the copyright of Dylan Thomas. Reprinted by permission of David Higham Associates Ltd and New Directions Publishing Corporation.

'How long does it take to make the woods?' from Sabbaths, Wendell Berry (North Point Press).

'London Trees' from Collected Poems, Kathleen Raine (Hamish Hamilton Ltd).

'Maple and Sumach' from Poems of C. Day Lewis 1925-72, C. Day Lewis (Jonathan Cape Ltd).

'The Song of the Open Road' from Collected Verse from 1929,

copyright Ogden Nash, printed by permission of Curtis Brown, London on behalf of the estate of Ogden Nash.

'The Thicket' from In the New District, Michael Vince (Carcanet Press).

'Trees' from Sibyls and Others, Ruth Fainlight (Hutchinson.).

'The Trees' from High Windows, Philip Larkin. Reprinted by permission of Faber & Faber Ltd.

'Winter Trees' from Collected Poems, Sylvia Plath (Faber & Faber) London. Copyright Ted Hughes 1971 and 1981 by permission of Olwyn Hughes.

'The Wooden-Shouldered Tree is Wild and High' from Collected Poems 1955-1975 Peter Levi (Anvil Press Poetry)

And to the Grigson family for 'Elms Under Cloud' by Geoffrey Grigson from the Collected Works of Geoffrey Grigson 1924-1962 Phoenix House 1963 (© Geoffrey Grigson 1963)

THANKS TO JO AND MIKE PARTON FOR GIV~ ING ME THE TIME.

TO-DAY THE HE PUTS FORTH TENDER LEAVES OF HOPE

WILLIAM SHAKESPEARE
KING HENRY VIII